KASHMIR

KASHMIR

Garden of the Himalayas

Introduction and 78 color photographs by

RAGHUBIR SINGH

Preface from the writings of Jawaharlal Nehru

THAMES AND HUDSON

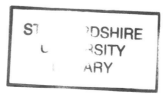

Photographs copyright © 1983 by Raghubir Singh
Introduction copyright © 1983 by Raghubir Singh
Writings of Jawaharlal Nehru copyright © 1981 by Rajiv Gandhi
Photographic layout by Raghubir Singh

First published in the United States in 1983 by
Thames and Hudson Inc., 500 Fifth Avenue,
New York, New York 10110

First paperback edition 1987   **03609961**

Library of Congress Catalog Card Number 83-70405

Printed and bound in Japan by Dai Nippon

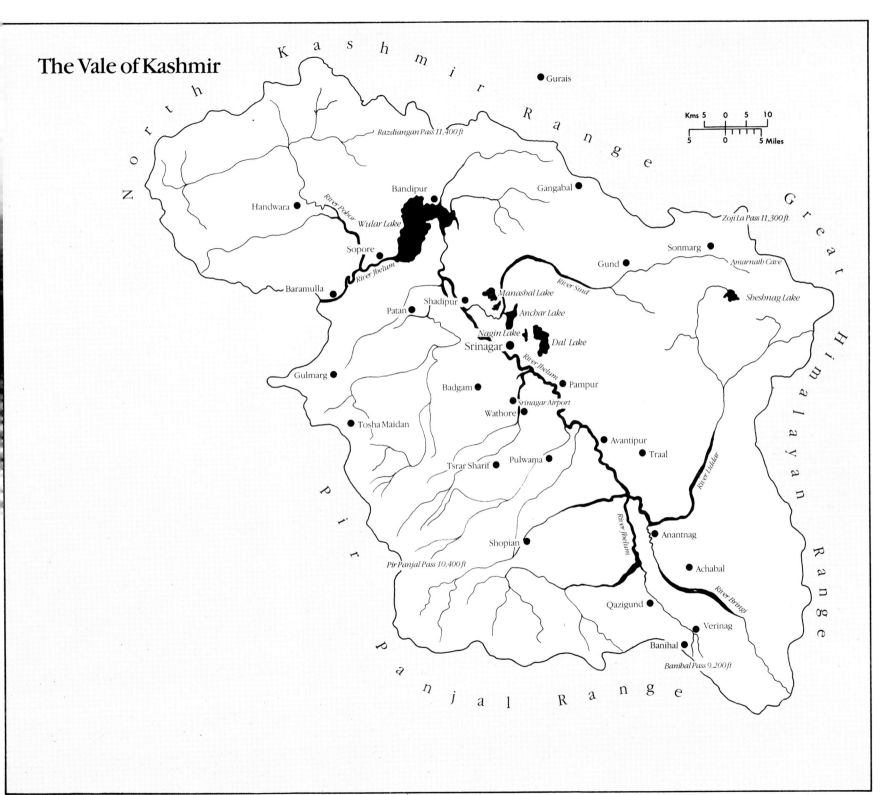

The Vale of Kashmir

- Gurais
- North Kashmir Range
- *Razdiangan Pass 11,400 ft*
- Bandipur
- Gangabal
- Handwara
- *River Pohor*
- *Wular Lake*
- Sopore
- *Zoji La Pass 11,300 ft.*
- Sonmarg
- Gund
- *Amarnath Cave*
- Baramulla
- *River Jhelum*
- *River Sind*
- Shadipur
- *Manashal Lake*
- *Sheshnag Lake*
- Patan
- *Anchar Lake*
- *Nagin Lake*
- Srinagar
- *Dal Lake*
- *Great Himalayan Range*
- Gulmarg
- *River Jhelum*
- Badgam
- Pampur
- *Srinagar Airport*
- Wathore
- Tosha Maidan
- Avantipur
- Traal
- Tsrar Sharif
- Pulwama
- *River Liddar*
- Shopian
- *River Jhelum*
- Anantnag
- *Pir Panjal Pass 10,400 ft*
- Achabal
- *River Bringi*
- Qazigund
- Verinag
- Banihal
- *Banihal Pass 9,200 ft*
- *Pir Panjal Range*

Kms 5 0 5 10
5 0 5 Miles

Acknowledgments

I would like to thank the following persons for their encouragement and kindness in the making of this book and during my various visits to Kashmir: Afzal Abdulla, Shameem Abdulla, Ghulam Qadir Basmati, Motilal Kemu, Subhana Badyari, Dr. Romila Thapar, Mala and Jugnu Singh, Ashok Jaitley, William Gedney, Bruce Palling, and Sally Holkar. The quote from Jawaharlal Nehru's *An Autobiography* (which begins his essay), and the excerpted essay from the *National Herald* newspaper of 24–31 July 1940, are used with the kind courtesy of Srimati Indira Gandhi and the Jawaharlal Nehru Memorial Fund.

Jawaharlal Nehru on Kashmir

We were Kashmiris. Over two hundred years ago, early in the eighteenth century, our ancestor came down from that mountain valley to seek fame and fortune in the rich plains below.

> Yea, in my mind these mountains rise,
> Their perils dyed with evening's rose;
> And still my ghost sits at my eyes
> And thirsts for their untroubled snows.

Nearly six years ago I quoted these lines from Walter de la Mare as I sat in prison writing the story of my life and thinking of my last visit to Kashmir. In prison or outside, Kashmir haunted me, and, though many years had passed since I had set eyes on its valleys and mountains, I carried the impress of them on the tablets of my mind. I yearned to visit them again, and struggled against this yearning. Was I to leave my work that took all my time, play truant to it, to satisfy the hunger of my eyes and the desire of my heart?

Friends in Kashmir invited me repeatedly to go there. Sheikh Abdullah pressed me again and again, and everyone who was of Kashmir reminded me that I, too, was a son of this noble land and owed a duty to it. I smiled at their insistence, for the urge within me was far greater than any that they could have placed before me.

I took the route via Abbottabad and the Jhelum Valley, a pleasant route with the panorama of the valley slowly unfolding in all its charm and beauty. But perhaps it would have been better if I had gone via Jammu and over the Pir Panjal. This is dull going most of the way, but as one crosses the mountain and goes through a long tunnel the sight that meets the eye is overpowering in its magic beauty. Out of the darkness one comes into the light, and there, far below, lies the vale of Kashmir, like some wonderland of our dreams, encircled by high mountains that guard it jealously from intrusion.

I did not go this way, and my approach was more sober and the change was slower. But my mind was filled with the excitement of my return, and it pleased me to be welcomed everywhere as a brother and a comrade, who in spite of long absence, was still of Kashmir and was coming back to his old homeland. With joy I saw the reality of the pictures in my mind which I had treasured for long years. I emerged from the mountains and the narrow valley, down which the Jhelum roared and tumbled in

7

youthful abandon, and the vale itself spread out before me. There were the famous poplars, slim and graceful sentinels, beckoning a welcome to you. There was the lordly chenar in all its majesty, with centuries of growth behind it. And there were the beautiful women and bonny children of Kashmir working in the fields.

We approached Srinagar, and there were cordial welcome and friendly faces everywhere. Up the river we went in a stately barge with numerous shikaras following, and the riverside steps and houses filled with cheering men and women and children. I was moved, as I have seldom been, by this affection that was showered upon me, and I became tongue-tied by the emotions that surged within me as the panorama of Srinagar passed by. Hari Parbat was in the background, and Shankaracharya or Takht-e-Suleiman loomed in the distance. I was in Kashmir.

I spent twelve days in Kashmir, and during this brief period we went some way up the Amarnath Valley and also the Liddar Valley to the Kolahoi glacier. We visited the ancient temple at Martand and sat under the venerable chenar trees at Brijbehara, which had grown and spread during four hundred years of human history. We loitered in the Moghul gardens and lived for a while in their scented past. We drank the delightful water of Chasme Shahi and swam about in the Dal Lake. We saw the lovely handiwork of the gifted artisans of Kashmir. We attended numerous public functions, delivered speeches, and met people of all kinds.

I tried to give my mind to the activity of the moment, and perhaps, in a measure, succeeded. But my mind was largely elsewhere, and I went through my engagements and the day's programme, and functioned on the public stage, like one who is absorbed in some other undertaking or is on a secret errand whose object he cannot disclose. The loveliness of the land enthralled me and cast an enchantment all about me. I wandered about like one possessed and drunk with beauty, and the intoxication of it filled my mind.

Like some supremely beautiful woman, whose beauty is almost impersonal and above human desire, such was Kashmir in all its feminine beauty of river and valley and lake and graceful trees. And then another aspect of this magic beauty would come to view, a masculine one, of hard mountains and precipices, and snow-capped peaks and glaciers, and cruel and fierce torrents rushing down to the valleys below. It had a hundred faces and innumerable aspects, ever-changing, sometimes smiling, sometimes sad and full of sorrow. The mist would creep up from the Dal Lake and, like a transparent veil, give glimpses of what was behind. The clouds would throw out their arms to embrace a mountain-top, or creep down stealthily like children at play. I watched this ever-changing spectacle, and sometimes the sheer loveliness of it was overpowering and I felt faint. As I gazed at it, it seemed to me dream-like and unreal, like the hopes and desires that fill us and so seldom find fulfilment. It was like the face of the beloved that one sees in a dream and that fades away on awakening.

Kashmir, even more than the rest of India, is a land of contrasts. In this land, overladen with natural beauty and rich nature's gifts, stark poverty reigns and humanity is continually struggling for the barest of subsistences. The men and women of Kashmir are good to look at and pleasant to talk to. They are intelligent and clever with their hands. They have a rich and lovely country to live in. Why, then should they be so terribly poor?

Again and again, as I was wrapped in pleasurable contemplation of Kashmir's beauty, I came back to hard earth with a shock when I saw this appalling poverty. Why should these people remain so miserably poor, I wondered, when nature had so abundantly endowed them?

I wish that some great architect would take charge of the planning and rebuilding of Srinagar. The river fronts should be attacked first of all, the slums and dilapidated houses should be removed and airy dwellings and avenues take their place, a proper drainage system introduced, and so much else done to convert Srinagar into a fairy city of dreamlike beauty, through which runs the Vitastha and the many canals sluggishly wind their way with the shikaras plying on them and the houseboats clinging to the banks. This is no fancy picture, for fairyland lies all round it; the magic is there already, but unfortunately human hands and human folly have tried to cover it here and there. Still it peeps out through slum and dirt.

We spent three and a half days in Srinagar and then sought a week's respite in the higher valleys. The vale itself and the gardens and country round Srinagar could have held me indefinitely, but I hungered for the mountains and the narrow paths over precipices and the glaciers. I wanted to crowd as much of experience and sensations as I could during these few days, to fill the storehouse of my memory with a picture gallery which I could visit at leisure when I chose to. Srinagar was also, inevitably, too full of engagements and interviews and meetings; it repeated too much the old pattern of any life.

We went on horseback and on foot. Some of our party did not like this trip because of the rain, and returned tired, bored, and exhausted. But I felt exhilarated by the beating of the rain on my face, and I loved to watch the rushing mountain torrent, whose winding course we followed. Leaving the party at Chandanwari, I went on some miles farther up with a friend. To my great regret, we could not go, for lack of time, to the lovely mountain lake of Shishnag, which was the next stage on the journey to the cave of Amarnath.

The weather had cleared and we scanned the skies hopefully and anxiously, for the next day we were to go to the Kolahoi glacier. During this trip to the Kolahoi there were a number of small accidents, and almost every member of our party had a fall from horseback or on boulders, or on the glacier itself. I was one of the fortunate few who escaped.

Back to Srinagar. Packing and leave-taking, a party at the Amar Singh Club, where I met many old friends, and a final public meeting to bid good-bye to the people of Srinagar.

The next morning we left Srinagar and sped towards Jammu. The road left the valley and mounted up the Pir Panjal. As we went higher, the panorama spread out before us and broader vistas came to view. We stood near the mouth of the tunnel and had a last look at the valley below. There lay the Vale of Kashmir, so famous in song and history, in its incomparable loveliness. A thin mist covered part of it, and a soft light toned down the hard edges of the picture. Above the clouds rose snow-capped peaks, and down from the valley below came the faint and distant sound of running water. We bade a silent farewell, and, turning away with regret, entered the dark tunnel which took us to less favoured lands.

Twelve days in Kashmir, twelve days after three-and-twenty years. Yet one vital moment is worth more than years of stagnation and vegetation, and to spend twelve days in Kashmir was good fortune indeed. But Kashmir calls back, its pull is stronger than ever, it whispers its fairy magic to the ears, and its memory disturbs the mind. How can they who have fallen under its spell release themselves from this enchantment?

(Excerpted from Jawaharlal Nehru, *An Autobiography*, Oxford University Press and Jawaharlal Nehru Memorial Fund, New Delhi; and from the *National Herald*, New Delhi, 24–31 July 1940)

Introduction

One hot summer day when I was six years old, my mother opened the refrigerator, and pointed to the ice compartment and below it to the pears and the plums. She exclaimed: "This is Kashmir!" In our home at Jaipur, the capital city of the arid state of Rajasthan, every scorching summer our thoughts, like those of innumerable Indians, would turn to the cool heights of the Himalayas. From antiquity to the age of the computer, countless Indians have been beguiled by Kashmir, a land of learning as well as of lakes and lofty mountains.

Our hot and dusty house contained a great many Kashmiri objects. In the living room, fleet-winged kingfishers and nimble golden orioles were deftly painted on lampshades and lampstands. Chinar leaves, chiselled on walnut tables, hinted at the mellow golds and burnished browns of the Kashmiri autumn. Our carpets, through their floral patterns, suggested the flowers and the fountains of the Moghul gardens. Every winter my mother would add to my child's vision of the Vale, when she wrapped herself in her Kashmiri shawl to keep away the chill winds blowing from the Himalayas, 300 miles to the north.

From 1965 to 1982 I was drawn to mountain-ringed Kashmir a dozen times, spending more than a dozen months there over the years. Thus I came to know its four seasons and much of its soil. When I first arrived, in the winter, the weather was dull and dreary. Day after day the sky was liquid. It snowed in the high Himalayas and sleet fell in Srinagar. I walked through the old quarters on the Jhelum River, a maze of narrow alleys with open sewers below brick and wood houses. Kashmiris shrouded in *pherans* carried under these cloaks *kangris*, small wicker-work baskets of burning coal, adding a mysterious touch to the mist-laden medieval city. One night an inch of snow transformed the unhealthy town into a magic place. But it was a short spell, almost an illusion. A day later the snow melted and I left for the warmth of the Indian Plain.

However, I returned to see the sparkle of spring, when nature rushes to bedeck the land with blossom after blossom: almond, apple, cherry, peach and pear. Violets, pansies, narcissi, crocuses and daisies burst into bloom. In the graveyards, the irises were an explosion of purple and white. This was the time I drove to the Wular Lake. There, rivulets lined with poplars, willows and mustard emptied into it. On the Dal Lake nothing was more restful than a ride in a *shikara*, the Kashmiri gondola. I was rowed through canals, past floating gardens and under Moghul bridges, where the white-breasted kingfishers plunged for their catch. I left the Vale through the Banihal road. From its height I saw the ripening rice-fields spread out for miles. The land glowed with the opulence of an enormous emerald.

When I came again in the summer the snows had melted on the mountains, leaving a touch of white on the topmost crags. The poplars had lost their freshness. The lotus buds opened rose-pink on Manasbal Lake. It was hot. Seeking the comfort of the Himalayan trails, I trekked to the 12,000-foot-high Sheshnag, the legendary lake named after the Lord of the Serpents who was supposed to dwell there. I camped above it for four days while hundreds of Hindus came to pay their homage to the *Nag* (the sacred snake): the guardian of the nether world, the constant companion of Vishnu, worn by Siva as a girdle, also considered as a symbol of eternity. For hours the devout scanned the turquoise surface of Sheshnag for a sight of the serpent.

I turned my attention to a book I carried in my back-pack, the seventh-century Sanskrit work, the *Nilmata Purana*, a manual in verse about the Vale's sacred spots, its rituals and its myths – one of its earliest cultural records. One passage is embedded in my mind: "Clad in blue raiment and possessed of blue eyes, O Nīla, O lord of the Nagas, even a man of unrestrained senses who contemplates you . . . is saved by your grace." Down by the lake, a group of excited sadhus told me they had seen the sacred snake. But I saw only reflections of wisps of floating cloud, patches of blue sky, sections of the sea-green mountain sides and the soft hues of dusk and dawn. These were ethereal enough. To me Sheshnag is the symbol of Kashmir's prehistoric past, when the whole Vale was a lake and even further back in time, eons ago, when the Himalayas rose out of the sea.

It was August. The auspicious full moon would shine in two days, the time it would take to walk from Sheshnag to the 13,000-foot-high Amarnath Cave. I joined the 20,000 pilgrims who had come from the ends of India to worship Siva the Creator, in his ice-phallic form as a *Shivling*, a stalagmite. On the way there, an endless line of the faithful silently filed past the glaciers which shimmered in the moonlight. But in the grotto I was almost trampled. A frantic mob tried to force its way to the divine symbol. The Kashmiri police, using barricades and long metal-tipped sticks, barely controlled the crush. I managed to catch a glimpse of the rose petal-covered *Shivling*. Then, with the words *"Har, Har, Mahadev!"* ("Victory to Siva!") ringing in my ears, I was pushed out into the open. In the bright Himalayan sunshine I saw fulfilment written on the faces of those who had done their worship. The sight of the *Shivling* had touched their souls, transforming the fire and the frenzy into satisfaction and serenity.

Summer gave way to autumn. The air of the Vale had a faint touch of withering flowers and foliage. Nature packed up for the season with wild abandon, spattering the scene with the honeyed yellow of the sunflower, the deep purple of saffron and the ember-like glow of the chinar – the Oriental plane tree.

In this mellow mood, I was held captive by two Moghul gardens. At the Nishat, I climbed a progression of terraces to view languid Dal Lake, the mist-wrapped Pir Panjals, and Hari Parbat – the hill formed when the goddess Parvati dropped a pebble to destroy a demon. And nearby Shalimar charmed me with its chinar-covered intimacy. There, around Shah Jehan's black marble pavilion, I saw Kashmiris picnic with wicker hampers and smoking samovars, before tumbling cascades, swift water-courses and fountains sending up plumes of water. The Kashmiris were happy in their heritage of Shalimar's perfumed past as they listened to the music of the falling water.

The spectacular sights, the sounds and the seasons had attached me to the life and landscape of Kashmir. I had come to like the sharp and sensitive Kashmiris whose complex character has been tempered by time on the anvil of Brahmanism and Buddhism, Saivism and Sufism, and above all moulded by the encircling Himalayas and the countless caravans of traders which have traversed the Vale for more than a thousand years. A look at the Vale's unique cockpit position in the heart of Asia, further north than Tibet, and at its considerable trade and unusual history is essential to understanding the Kashmiris.

The original state of Jammu and Kashmir consisted of several diverse regions: Baltistan, Dardistan, Muzaffarabad, Mirpur, Poonch, Jammu, Ladakh, the Vale of Kashmir and other mountainous tracts. The entire polyglot and heterogeneous territory is often inaccurately called Kashmir. Strictly speaking, only the Vale is Kashmir. There the Moslems make up 94 per cent of its population. There a distinctive history, geography, language and culture, shared by its Moslems and its Kashmiri Hindus, provide a sense of continuity and character.

Kashmir's homogeneous character has been created by its strategic and mountain-locked position on the southern periphery of Central Asia. The mile-high Vale sits in

the lap of the lesser Himalayas towering to 18,000 feet. This immense irregular oval, 84 miles in length and 20 to 25 miles in breadth, is divided by the Jhelum River, into which flow a host of tributaries from interlocking side valleys. The Vale is the gift of the Jhelum. This fertile land lies at the crossroads of the ancient mercantile trails connecting the Punjab and the Indo-Gangetic Plain with the Silk Roads of Central Asia. I set out to travel to some of the twenty-six gateways and traditional trade routes which have been so vital to Kashmir.

Through one of the side valleys, on the north-east, I followed the swift-flowing Sind. Shortly after Sonmarg, the tree-line recedes, the road snakes away from the river in steep and sharp bends and climbs slowly up until it reaches the pass, the 11,300-foot-high snow-streaked Zoji La. This was traditionally the great gateway to Central Asia.

Through Ladakh, Leh and the Indus furrow, the traders travelled to and fro from Khotan, Yarkand, Kashgar and other trading posts on the ancient arteries of communication connecting China with the Mediterranean lands. The Sino-Indian war of 1962 closed this age-old commerce to "innermost Asia".

Later I explored two lesser corridors to Central Asia. On the north, skirting the shores of Wular Lake, I drove over the 11,400-foot-high Razdiangan Pass to the Valley of Gurais; and on the north-west, I followed the road through the narrow Jhelum gorge to the town of Uri. From remote times to the mid-nineteenth century, restless and rapacious tribesmen made these two passages unsafe for regular trade. In our own century, the Indo-Pakistan war of 1947 terminated all traffic for the time being.

On the south are two major gateways. The first, the lifeline to the Indian Plain, is today an all-weather road through the Jawahar Tunnel (named after Nehru) which pierces the Pir Panjals 1,500 feet below the 9,000-foot-high Banihal Pass. The second is still a medieval trail through the Pir Panjal Pass. It was once called the Salt Route,* because that essential commodity was carried to Kashmir from the Punjab. Over it a French physician, François Bernier,** journeyed to Kashmir in the seventeenth century. He accompanied the Emperor Aurangzeb's regal entourage, composed of thousands of

* Also known as the Moghul or Imperial Route.
** François Bernier: *Travels in the Mogul Empire, AD 1656–1668*, edited by Archibald Constable, London 1981, p. 407.

foot soldiers and cavalry, hundreds of heavy guns, fifteen to thirty thousand porters and a procession of womenfolk on elephants. Bernier tells us fifteen of the pachyderms stampeded near a precipice and fell to their death.

Over Kashmir's many mountain passes came Moghul monarchs, mercenaries and, most of all, caravans of merchants. The monumental Sanskrit poem and chronicle of Kashmir, Kalhana's *Rajatarangini*, the River of Kings (the earliest surviving history of India, 1148–49), refers repeatedly to the lucrative commerce of Kashmir. In one place the historian tells us: "... [the] land, which was full of merchants of different wares, come from all regions ..."* And over the centuries the trading genius of the Kashmiris continued to develop. Six hundred years later the Scotsman John Bogle, after travelling to Tibet for the English East India Company, echoed and enlarged Kalhana's observations. He wrote, "Many foreign merchants ... have settled in Tibet. The natives of Kashmir who, like the Jews in Europe or the Armenians in the Turkish Empire, scatter themselves over the eastern kingdoms of Asia ... Their agents, stationed on the coast of the Coromandel, in Bengal, in Benares, Nepal and Kashmir, furnish them with the commodities of these different countries ..."** Throughout their history the Kashmiris have ranked among the foremost traders of the subcontinent.

The important items of the Vale's ancient and medieval trade, though dependent on supply and demand, remained unchanged for centuries. Saffron, shawls, silks, blankets, and aromatic costus were the principal exports. Shawl-wool, silver, salt, spices, drugs, tea, tobacco, cotton goods, gold, precious stones and ponies were the principal imports. Moreover, there were those articles which Kashmiris carried directly between India and Central Asia.

Sometimes a single article could transform the Vale's economy. Kashmiri shawls woven from *pashmina* and *shahtush*, the latter being the finest and warmest but rare, were prized by centuries of Moghuls and Maharajas. Through the trade routes the shawl had reached the land of the Nile. And through Napoleon's Egyptian campaign (1798–1801) it became an item of fashion in France. The Empress Josephine possessed between three and four hundred "*châles et dentelles*". Each was bought for 1,700 to

* M. A. Stein: *Kalhana's Rājatarangini: A Chronicle of the Kings of Kashmir*, London 1900, vol. 1, bk. 4, p. 121.
** John Bogle quoted by John MacGregor: *Tibet, A Chronicle of Exploration*, London 1970, p. 149.

3,000 francs. According to one story, Napoleon liked to see Josephine's shoulders bared. Often he pulled off her shawl and flung it into the fire, whereupon the Empress would calmly send for another one.*

By the middle of the nineteenth century, however, a Jacquard loom-woven imitation had appeared, leading in twenty years to the mass-produced Paisley. This shawl cost only £1, making it popular among the European middle classes. Consequently, the wealthier classes gradually abandoned the exotic and original *kashmirs*. At the same time, the Franco-Prussian War (1870–71) resulted in the closure of the French market. In Kashmir this war was watched with anxiety by the shawl-weavers, who burst into tears and loud lamentations when news of the French defeat reached them. In the heyday of the shawl there were 11,000 looms and 28,000 weavers in the Vale, whose population was 800,000.** Now there are more weavers and looms, but the shawl is no longer a major export.

What the shawl was to nineteenth-century Kashmir, the apple is to present-day Kashmir. The apple-rich village of Naupura, commonly called *Chota* or Little London, lies on the outskirts of Sopore, the centre of the apple industry, and resembles a suburb of Srinagar. The streets are unpaved but the houses are tin-roofed and brick-walled. Ghulam Mohammed Parimau, a resident, told me, "Twelve years ago this was a village of mud huts, now everyone owns a car, a telephone and a television set. The apple trade has brought us wealth. Much of the money earned is used to acquire more orchards." A nine-million-rupee (*c.* £560,000) apple-grading project has been launched in the village with the assistance of the Australian Government, and other large-scale horticultural development schemes are being undertaken.

The planting of new varieties of apples, like the fast-growing Delicious and the American, sparked the boom. In nearby Baramulla, a leading businessman and orchard owner, 63-year-old Inayatullah Kakru, talked to me nostalgically about the Amri, an older brand. He said: "It has almost disappeared. It took long to ripen but its bouquet could fill a room." According to Kakru, Kashmiri farmers marketed a total of 400,000 tons of fresh fruit in 1981. (The second largest product is timber, of which 130,000 tons were sold in the same year.)

* John Irwin, *Shawls: A Study in Indo-European Influences*, London 1955, pp. 32–36.
** Walter Lawrence, *Valley of Kashmir*, London 1895, p. 377.

Seventy per cent of the Vale's three million inhabitants live in villages. Rice is their staple diet, and the growing of paddy and the tending of orchards takes up much of their time. They also grow smaller cash crops like oilseeds, vegetables and saffron, and more than two million mulberry trees provide a subsidiary income for thousands of farmers.

A variety of handicrafts are another essential to the rural welfare, especially in the dark winter days when the farmers cannot work in the fields. Between 1977 and 1981, 30,000 new artisans were trained through a major programme. In the villages and the towns there are over 150,000 craftsmen producing papier-mâché, carpets, shawls, silverware, embroidery, rugs, imitation jewellery, wicker-willow and wood-carving. These attractive articles are sold all over India and abroad.

But the Indo-Kashmiri interdependence is marked by suspicion. To Indians the word Kashmiri characterizes cunning. The Kashmiris in turn complain about the overbearing attitude of an overwhelming number of Indians. The Kashmiris do not care to improve their image, nor do Indians care to question their prejudice. Yet, however much the Kashmiris may dislike the Indians, they know the latter are vital to the Vale's economy. In 1981, 550,000 Indians took their vacations in the Vale, while only 44,000 foreigners came there.

Kashmir is tied to India by two of the softest strands of *shahtush*: an article of the Indian Constitution which gives the State a special status whereby its people have a measure of autonomy; and a law which restricts ownership of property to citizens of Jammu and Kashmir. Kashmiris prize these privileges. Such concessions are compatible with their essentially pacific disposition, which is rooted in their thousand-year-old passion for commerce, but history has rarely been kind to them.

An important part of Kashmiri history is portrayed in a series of folk plays, the *Bhand Paither*, performed for centuries by the Bhands, a community of performing artists. These popular plays on the Afghans, the Moghuls, the English and others, like the Dards from Dardistan – Kashmir's northern neighbours – depict the tyrannies inflicted on the Kashmiris for over five hundred years. Through satire, slapstick, puns and proverbs, they reveal the Kashmiri spirit of submission.

Wathore is one of the many Bhand villages. It is sixteen miles from Srinagar, on the road to the shrine of Tsrar Sharif, and directly in the flightpath of the tourist-laden

Airbus and Boeing jets flying in and out of the airport. Yet Wathore is worlds away from modernity. Huts with mud walls and thatch roofs haphazardly huddle between walnut, peach, pear and pomegranate trees abutting groves of willows. Majestic chinars shade some of the settlement. A muddy stream, with ducks waddling in it, winds its way through clusters of houses interspersed by rice-fields. On an earthen embankment stands a small shrine, the ubiquitous *ziarat* of the Kashmiri village.

A festival is taking place. The shrine is surrounded by makeshift shops selling cakes, breads, sherbets, sweetmeats, shoes, slippers, bangles, clay pots, metal utensils, axes and simple farming implements. Knots of villagers huddle around quacks selling aphrodisiacs and charms. The children are occupied by a variety of games: shooting at balloons, carousing on crude merry-go-rounds, throwing hoops and knocking down tin cans with a rubber ball. Bombay film music blares from a loudspeaker.

Caught in the crush of the crowd, I drift towards a slope overlooking an opening in a clump of trees where a folk-play is about to begin. The film music abruptly ends and the *Dard Paither* is announced. The performance starts with three Bhands blowing on the *surnai* (the folk-oboe), playing fast and repetitive rhythms, accompanied by a pair of *nagara* (kettle drums) and a *dhol* (a two-headed, barrel-shaped drum). The musicians herald a row of dancers. They are followed by a procession led by the haughty Dard king who doesn't even speak Kashmiri. Dressed in brocade and accompanied by two wives, he gets drunk, beats and bullies the people – symbolized by clowns in sackcloth. The whip is often used in the *Paither* as an object of oppression. After being lashed, a clown comments, ''I don't feel the pain. I am used to it. There is nothing new in it.'' Finally, the exasperated clowns kidnap the two queens. The Dard king flees.

Kashmir has been ruled by foreigners, such as the Dards, through most of its history. Often Kashmiris themselves invited foreign rule. Our knowledge of the early history of Kashmir is sketchy, since the premier source, Kalhana's chronicle, is inaccurate for that period. But we do know that Buddhism was brought to the Vale by missionaries dispatched by the great Indian Emperor Ashoka (269–232 BC), while it was under his sphere of influence. When the Kushan king, Kanishka, ruled Kashmir in the first century or early second century AD, he convened there a six-month-long Buddhist council which resulted in the foundation of Mahayana Buddhism. Thereafter Kashmiri missionaries were the foremost in spreading the doctrine to Central Asia, China and later to Java. In the fifth century a ruthless Hun sought shelter in the Vale, usurped the throne and tyrannized the people until he was murdered.

The Vale's history assumes a more authentic character during the reign of the Hindu Karkota kings, in the seventh and eighth centuries. Lalitaditya (724–61) was the outstanding Karkota king and Kashmir's greatest Hindu monarch. He favoured the two prominent faiths: Buddhism and Brahmanism. He liberally patronized learning. He sent cultural missions abroad and invited scholars to study in Kashmir. Kashmiri bronze sculpture attained an artistic peak. Public services were reorganized, charitable institutions were set up and towns and temples built. This was a rare period for Kashmir, an era of expansion and conquest, when the Punjab came under Lalitaditya's control and his rule reached the Gangetic Plain. Kashmiri historians, mixing fact and fable, credit him with an overwhelming area of conquest from Central Asia to Central India. However, other historians, though conceding his great signi cance, qualify Lalitaditya's role as a conqueror. S. C. Ray, in his *Early History and Culture of Kashmir*, writes that during the reign of an earlier Karkota king "China supplied military aid to Kashmir. In Lalitaditya's time she [Kashmir] depended on Chinses help to fight the Tibetans. . . . It is apparent that Kashmir as a subordinate ally assisted China in her enterprises in that region. . . . So long as the Tang dynasty was in power, she evinced great strength. But with the decline of the Tangs . . . Kashmir is no longer seen to carry on a policy of expansion. She retired from the scene, never to appear again.''*

The Karkota kings gave Kashmir its first majestic monuments. The Sun Temple of Martand, built by Lalitaditya, set the style for the Vale's Hindu architecture. The ruins of Avantivarman's (855–83) grand capital city lie 18 miles south of Srinagar. In this period, difficult feats of engineering were undertaken. Embankments and dams were built on the fast-flowing rivers.

However, the next four hundred years, from the tenth to the fourteenth centuries, were a time of treason and treachery and oppression in Kashmir, with rare respites. There rose in the Vale rival bodies of troops with powerful commanders, as well as feudal barons who became kingmakers. The chiefs of the adjacent hill tract of Lohara also began to play a prominent part in the Vale's politics, with the result that they

* S. C. Ray: *Early History and Culture of Kashmir*, Calcutta 1958, p. 54.

finally formed their own dynasty there. In these troubled times, it was not surprising that ambitious and ruthless outsiders were attracted to the Vale.

In the twelfth century, a descendant of Genghis Khan plundered Kashmir. But with the approach of winter, he tried to leave the Vale through the Banihal Pass and perished in a blizzard. Shortly afterwards, Rinchana, a Tibetan prince, usurped the throne. Kashmiris believe that Rinchana was the first ruler to popularize Islam in Kashmir. They say he asked the Brahmins to convert him to Hinduism, but when the request was refused, he vowed to follow the faith of the next person he saw. This chanced to be a Transonian Moslem mystic. Many courtiers and a part of the populace followed Rinchana's example and converted to Islam. In the meantime, another adventurer, Shah Mir, a native of Swat, had arrived in the Vale, and in due course entered the service of Rinchana. When the latter died, Shah Mir seized the kingdom and in 1338 founded the Sultan dynasty in Kashmir.

The most celebrated Sultan and ruler of Kashmir was Zain-ul-Abidin, popularly known as Badshah or Great King. During his enlightened rule, from 1420 to 1470, he reversed the bigoted politics of his predecessor, Sikander the iconoclast. He showed a keen interest in Hindu and Buddhist philosophy and patronized prose, poetry, dance and music. He introduced new arts like shawl embroidery, carpetmaking, papier-mâché, silverwork and metalwork, and sent craftsmen to Persia and Samarkand on scholarships. He was the Akbar of Kashmir and a precursor of that remarkable Moghul monarch by a hundred years. Badshah was succeeded by a line of weak Sultans. The throne changed hands eighteen times in less than a century. Then a group of Shiites from Dardistan grabbed Sunni Kashmir. But their rule was a thirty-year interlude marked by religious rifts which led to Moghul intervention.

In 1587 Kashmir was merged into the Moghul Empire. Two years later Akbar visited the Vale and declared it "my private garden". This "pearl of Hind" enjoyed peace and prosperity during Moghul rule. Numerous land reforms were introduced. Akbar's son Jehangir was enchanted by Kashmir. During his reign (1605–27) the Vale was reputed to have 777 gardens, including the storied Shalimar. Jehangir wished to die and be buried in Kashmir but fate willed otherwise. In his memoirs he rhapsodized about the land he loved: "Kashmir is a garden of eternal spring, or an iron fort to a palace of kings – a delightful flower-bed, and a heart-expanding heritage for dervishes. Its pleasant meads and enchanting cascades are beyond all description. There are running streams and fountains beyond count. . . .''*

Shah Jehan (1627–58) was also beguiled by the garden of the Himalayas. He dismissed a governor on receiving reports of ruthlessness and cruelty. He introduced fresh laws and terminated unfair taxes. But with Aurangzeb's death in 1707, Moghul grandeur waned and the Empire disintegrated.

The oppressive Afghan occupation (1753–1819), which followed the benevolent Moghul rule, was one of the most tyrannical in Kashmir's history. The Afghans amassed wealth by any means. The following verse was popular at the time:

> God wanted that this blue-coloured land
> should tire of wailing like the reed's heart.
> He gave its control to the Afghan,
> He gave Jamshid's garden to the demons.**

Then famines struck the Vale. The worst occurred in 1773. The desperate Kashmiris petitioned the powerful Sikh ruler of the Punjab to intervene and end the atrocities of the Afghans. Ranjit Singh, who already had an eye on the Vale, immediately seized the opportunity. Sikh rule (1819–46), though not cruel, was harsh. The Sikhs spent much of their time fighting the tribesmen on the northern borders of the Vale.

Upon Ranjit Singh's death in 1839, the English stepped in. At that time they were consolidating their control over north India. They feared the Russian advance in Central Asia and coveted its commerce. After defeating the successors of Ranjit Singh, the East India Company turned over Kashmir to the Dogra ruler of Jammu for a modest sum. But according to an article of the treaty, the Dogra-Maharaja became a vassal of the Company. And as a token of British supremacy, he was "to present annually to the British Government one horse, twelve perfect shawl-goats of approved breed (six male and six female), and three pairs of Kashmiri shawls." It was the Hindu Dogras who amalgamated the modern state of Jammu and Kashmir. Their rule edged Kashmir towards the twentieth century.

* The *Tūzuk-i-Jahāngīrī* or *Memoirs of Jahāngīr*, translated by Alexander Rogers, edited by Henry Bevridge, London 1909, 1914, vol. 2, p. 143.
** G. L. Tikku: *Persian Poetry in Kashmir* (1339–1846), Berkeley, California 1971, p. 159.

In the 1930s a popular movement for political reform was launched, with Sheikh Abdullah as the guiding spirit. The son of a shawl-weaver, he was a school teacher and one of the first Kashmiri Moslems to study English. In 1946 the Sheikh started his "Quit Kashmir" campaign against the Dogra-Maharaja, who imprisoned him.

With the partition of India in August 1947, the Dogra ruler was in a dilemma. Could Jammu and Kashmir be independent or should it accede to India or to Pakistan? But a dramatic event ended his quandary. In late October Pakistani tribesmen, backed by military advisers in mufti, tried to take the Vale by force. But instead of quickly seizing Srinagar and the airport, they stopped to plunder, murder and rape. This invasion provoked the vacillating Dogra to accede to the Indian Union and ask for help to expel the invaders. Sheikh Abdullah, who had been released from prison, endorsed the decision. While accepting the Act of Accession, Lord Mountbatten, the Governor-General of India, added the proviso that the question of accession be determined by a State-wide referendum. Because of the events which followed, the plebiscite never took place.

A day later Indian troops were flown in and the Vale was saved. But the fighting went on for more than a year. Finally, under the supervision of the United Nations, India and Pakistan signed a cease fire agreement on 1 January 1949. Pakistan occupied 33,000 square miles of Jammu and Kashmir's original 86,500 square miles. The coveted Vale, along with Jammu and Ladakh, remained with India. UN troops patrolled the cease fire line. In 1954 Pakistan joined in a military pact with the United States and allowed an American airbase to be established at Gilgit in the occupied zone of the State. Thus Kashmir was thrown into the arena of Superpower politics. In the same year the democratically elected Jammu and Kashmir Legislative Assembly ratified the accession. From that time onwards, Jammu and Kashmir became an integral part of the Indian Union.

In 1965 Pakistan started its second war with India, by sending infiltrators into the Vale in the belief that the Kashmiris would actively aid their Moslem brethren. In 1971, during the third Indo-Pakistan war, heavy fighting took place in Kashmir; but in both wars the Kashmiris did nothing. They remained true to their history as passionate spectators but faint-hearted participants. To secular India, the country with the second largest Moslem population in the world (after Indonesia) and the world's most diverse Moslem community, Kashmir is crucial to its existence as a non-sectarian state.

The Kashmiri Hindu-Moslem relationship has traditionally been harmonious, with few examples of friction. The Kashmiri Moslems and the local Hindus, the Pandits, have through much of their history lived in an environment of accommodation. The thirty-five-year-long friendship of Sheikh Abdullah and Jawaharlal Nehru, a Pandit, underlines this bond. In spite of their deep differences, politics not religion was the divide. The Sheikh was a Kashmiri first and an Indian afterwards. He was a state politician with a vision. He had a vast following in the Vale and numerous admirers outside. On the other hand, Nehru's ancestors had migrated from the Vale to the Indian Plain. He was educated at Harrow and at Trinity College, Cambridge, grew up in an intellectual and international milieu, became the first Prime Minister of India and a world statesman. Yet, Kashmir was written across Nehru's heart. Both leaders needed each other and both believed in a secular India. About the Sheikh, Nehru wrote, "Sheikh Mohammad Abdullah was a real leader of the people . . . He was the founder and initiator of the [Kashmiri freedom] movement. At first it began on communal lines . . . But Sheikh Abdullah pulled it out of these ruts and had the courage and statesmanship to steer it out of the narrow waters of communalism into the broad sea of nationalism."* Nehru supported the Sheikh until political problems eroded their friendship, after the latter became the chief executive of Jammu and Kashmir. The Sheikh harboured visions of an independent Kashmir. His speeches were not politic. In Srinagar and New Delhi there were mandarins and powerful politicians who quickly seized the opportunity to manipulate and magnify the rift. As a result Sheikh Abdullah was arrested in 1953. He remained in the political wilderness for twenty-two years, thirteen of which were passed in detention. In 1964, Nehru, who had never reconciled himself to the Sheikh's arrest, ordered his release and sent him to Pakistan on an exploratory mission. There the Sheikh heard of Nehru's death. Heartbroken, he hurried immediately to New Delhi and attended the funeral of his friend with tears in his eyes. Eventually, in 1975, Nehru's daughter, Indira Gandhi, made an accord with the Sheikh who then became the Chief Minister of Jammu and Kashmir. He died in September 1982 in his position of power.

* Jawaharlal Nehru: *National Herald*, 24–31 July 1940.

In or out of power, for fifty long years, the Sheikh had been the principal protagonist of Kashmiri politics. Those men who ruled the State, in the interim, were men of neither substance nor stature. Sheikh Abdullah was a man who loved Kashmir and the Kashmiri people – Moslems, Hindus, Sikhs and Buddhists – with all his mind and heart. The Kashmiris returned this love and remained steadfastly loyal to him, in spite of accusations by his opponents of poor performance and corruption. The name Kashmiris gave this charismatic and courageous man, "the Lion of Kashmir", will rightfully endure.

On one visit to the Vale – the Sheikdom, as the Indian press often called it – in April 1979, I arrived two days after Zulfiqar Ali Bhutto, the ex-Prime Minister of Pakistan, was hanged by the repressive regime of General Zia ul-Haq. Bhutto was popular among India's Moslems and the execution started riots in Kashmir. My friend Ghulam Qadir Basmati, a taxi-driver and shopowner, met me at the airport. Though we expected some trouble, the drive into town was surprisingly easy. The main target of the protest was the *Jamaat-i-Islami*, a fundamentalist and pro-Pakistani politico-religious party. In many villages the houses and offices of the *Jamaat*'s workers and their sympathizers were damaged or destroyed. Four days later life in the Vale was back to normal. Basmati put it in a nutshell when he told me: "We produce more noise than blood, we abhor bloodshed. Our anger is quickly aroused but it also dissipates quickly."

However, there has been one five-week-long unusual upsurge in Kashmir. A strand of the Prophet's hair was brought to India in 1635 from Medina. Late in the seventeenth century it was carried to Kashmir and housed at Hazratbal, making it the Vale's most sacred shrine. On the night of 26–27 December 1963 the holy relic or the *Moe-e-Muqaddas* was stolen. All of Kashmir was shocked. Riots rocked the Vale. The State Government was paralysed and the ruling politicians and their property attacked. Even though it was bitterly cold – snow covered the land – villagers carrying bulky bedding, bundles of food and fuel flocked to Srinagar. There were long mourning processions with chants of "*Allah O Akbar*" and "*Ya Rasul Allah*" ("God is Great" and "O Messenger of God"), interspersed with cries of "Let us have the *Moe-e-Muqaddas* back!" Black flags flew from the tops of houses and vehicles. Housewives stopped cooking. Crowds kept a twenty-four-hour vigil at the shrine and in the streets, eating at roadside stalls. Hindus, Buddhists and Sikhs joined the upheaval. A thick fog cast a gloom over the Vale. Then, as mysteriously as it had disappeared, the relic was recovered on 4 January 1964. Shortly afterwards it was reinstalled in its sanctuary, verified by holy men and exhibited to a crowd of over 50,000 people.

The worship of the Holy Hair is a particularly non-Islamic practice. It attests to the Vale's Buddhist and mystic heritage. There are other relics revered in Kashmir, and shrines honouring Sufi saints dot the land. Many date back to the fourteenth century when 700 disciples of Shah Hamadan, a prominent Sufi from Persia, proselytized the people of the Vale, bringing them under the lasting impress of Moslem mysticism.

According to Alberuni, the medieval Moslem scholar, the word Sufi derives from the Greek term for wisdom: *sophia*. But the Arabic word for wool, *suf*, suggests the common interpretation of the origin of the cult: the early sages and ascetics wore coarse woollen garments and these habits, in the course of time, came to suggest penitence and piety.

There arose in Kashmir an indigenous order of Sufism, known as the Rishi order. It was founded by Sheikh Nur-ud-din or Nund Rishi (died 1438). The Rishis combined Buddhist renunciation, Hindu asceticism (especially the sayings of the fourteenth-century Saivite saint and poet-preacher Lalla) with traditional Sufism. The Rishis believed in the love of mankind and did not proselytize. Thus they were popular among Moslems as well as Hindus.

The hearing of harmonious sounds, i.e. poetry and music, leads the Sufis to intensify their sensations of love for God and transports them to a state of ecstasy in which they believe they experience communion with the Creator. In Kashmir this devotional music is known as *Sufiana Kalam*. To understand something of the "music of mystic content", I visited Mohammed Ghulam Qaleen Bhaff, at seventy years the oldest living master-musician. Through a narrow alley I entered his house in the old city of Srinagar. Bhaff's son let me in. We passed a small chamber filled by a loom. The son informed me that their family have been carpet-weavers for seven generations. He left me alone in a dimly lit room. A *santoor* (a trapezoidal zither) with its two very light wooden beaters and a pair of *dukras* (drums similar to the Indian *tabla*) lay in a corner. The *saz-i-Kashmir* (a plucked string instrument) was propped up against a wall. Before I could complete my survey of the room, the door opened and a tall, bearded and burly man with a long hook-nose, wearing a blue cotton skull cap and a grey *pheran* entered. Qaleen Bhaff and I greeted each other. His son brought him a hubble bubble and between puffs and gurgling sounds Bhaff talked to me about his art. He said: "It is an inseparable unity of poetry and music. It is food for the *fakir* [a Sufi holy man in Kashmir]. The listener is transported to another world. Even though a war may be going on, he will not be distracted. Such is the force of *Sufiana Kalam*."

Through a *fakir*, a carpenter by profession, I attended a *Sufiana Kalam* session near the famous shrine of Nund Rishi in the town of Tsrar Sharif. The room was filled with the soft sound of the *santoor* and the *saz*, the gentle beat of the *dukra* and the smell of burning incense. Men shrouded in blankets and shawls sat in a circle. A young man sang a succession of Persian verses. There were expressions of emotion and ecstasy on all faces. Some sang in chorus gesturing simultaneously, others were silent, their heads bowed in meditation. Still others, with eyes closed, slowly rocked their heads. One man's body shook. He was in a trance and repeatedly touched his forehead to the ground. Eventually a long break for lunch followed. After the meal the singing was resumed. I left late in the afternoon. The Sufis continued their poetic worship till dawn the next day.

Kashmir's mysticism is favoured by the masses but frowned upon by the fundamentalist *Jamaat-i-Islami*. Pir Sad-ud-din, the shrewd and sharp-eyed seventy-year-old head of this small but important organization told me, "The word Sufi is not in the Koran. The marginal Sufis, like Shah Hamadan, were true Moslems. Today Sufis add and detract from Islam. They ignore the five prayers a day. Shrines can be tolerated but not music, dance and theatre. We have to change the mental attitude of the people of Kashmir. Their knowledge of the Koran is poor. Their education is poor." I suspect the cunning and cautious Sad-ud-din does not dare to openly condemn Shah Hamadan the Sufi or the countless shrines because of their overwhelming popularity in Kashmir.

There is much about the Kashmiris which makes the *Jamaat* unhappy. Since 1947, when the *Jamaat* began their work in the Vale, their progress has been slow. They won only one seat in the last election (1977) to the State legislature. In the riots following Bhutto's death, their support dipped dramatically. But since then they have made a remarkable recovery. They run schools and also use study circles and mosques to propagate their fanaticism.

Their youth wing, the *Jamaat-i-Tulba*, advocates secession and revolution. Sheikh Tajammul Islam, its president, attempted to organize a meeting of the world's Islamic youth in Kashmir. Addressing the press on 5 August 1980, he declared, ". . . the basic topic of the conference will be *The Islamic Revolution in Kashmir . . .* The kind of revolution brought by Ayatollah Khomeini in Iran will be best for us." At his proposed gathering, it was believed Mr. Islam wanted unilaterally to declare Kashmir an Islamic nation; the late Sheikh Abdullah prohibited the convention and packed him off to jail.

I am not particularly concerned with the narrow world of the *Jamaat*. My real interest lies in the Vale's non-sectarian side, especially in its age-old liberal traditions of art and culture. There was a time when Kashmir was the home of Sanskrit scholarship and rivalled Benares as a centre of learning. Its Buddhist monks travelled the trade routes, those corridors of culture, to carry its Sanskrit civilization to Central Asia and China. Its scholars and sages wrote lasting literary works. The undated ancient classic on dance, drama and music, the *Natya Shastra*, was written in the Vale. Contemporary Indian dancers still abide by its theory of aesthetics. In the second century BC, Patanjali compiled his compendium on the Yoga, the earliest systematic study of the discipline. In the eleventh century AD, Somadeva Bhatta produced one of the epic masterpieces of the world, the *Katha-sarit-sagara*, the *Ocean of the Streams of Story*. Its 22,000 verses, plus prose, make it twice as long as the *Iliad* and the *Odyssey* together. These timeless tales were written for the amusement of a queen. The *Panchatantra*, a collection of tales and fables in prose and verse, goes back to the early centuries of the Christian era. Between the tenth and twelfth centuries Kashmir produced a remarkable range of Sanskrit literature, from Saivite philosophy to eroticism; surprisingly, a substantial number of these works were written during times of trouble and tension, when Hinduism was beginning to decay and decline in the Vale.

Later, when Islam replaced Hinduism, bringing with it the influences of Central Asia and Persia, the Kashmiris used the fruits of the fading Hindu-Buddhist civilization as a foundation to develop a distinctive and dynamic Moslem culture. One of the lasting results of this borrowing and blending was that the Kashmiris became masters in a variety of handicrafts. From medieval to modern times, the Vale has attracted the artisans of many lands.

A papier-mâché artist, who emigrated from Iran to Kashmir in the early twentieth century, was hired to decorate the wooden ceiling of the Durbar Hall of the Maharaja's palace on the Jhelum River in Srinagar. His son Mohammed Abdulla and grandson Afzal Abdulla are now among the Vale's most respected businessmen. They run Asia Crafts, the best shop and showplace for contemporary handicrafts.

They sent me to meet seventy-five-year-old Ghulam Hussain Mir who, though suffering from asthma and failing eyesight, had been working on a four-piece wooden screen for three years. As I admired the gold work on one finished section, he remarked: "The transfer of gold leaf is a difficult task. It cannot be done consistently hour after hour. I work only three to four hours a day." Then he described the process: "I got the screens cut from fir. I smoothed the wood with sandpaper and pasted on it one layer of tissue paper. Again I sandpapered the surface, glued a fine muslin over it and spread a thin coating of plaster of Paris which I polished with a stone. Again I pasted tissue paper and again I sandpapered the surface. Then, with a pencil, I drew the floral design. That done, I made *dhor*, a paste from sugar, salt, milk and gum, and applied it very evenly to get the gold leaf to bring out the details of the drawing. Any fault in applying the *dhor* would dull the lustre of the gold. It is used only in the morning when the air is moist and cool. I do not use the paste for the forty hot days from 1 July to 10 August." He paused and resumed his labour of love, which I watched till mid-morning, when he blew on a corner of the last gold leaf and tapped it in with the middle finger of his right hand. A vivid pattern of golden chinar leaves emerged. Now his toil was nearing an end. He would deftly paint the minutest details with four fast colours and finally the screen would be coated with four light veneers of varnish. Back in Asia Crafts, Afzal Abdulla told me: "Ghulam Hussain Mir is a master whose artistry is unmatched. Now Kashmir, not Iran, is the home of papier-mâché. However, in carpets they still hold an edge over us."

Afzal Abdulla was soon to be married, and he invited me to the wedding lunch. I looked forward to the *wazwan*, the elaborate Kashmiri meal made mostly from mutton. It is also eaten at births, circumcisions and religious occasions. About a thousand *wazas*, who specialize in the preparation of these meals, work in the Vale. In an area called Wazpura, they stock hundreds of huge copper cooking pots. The owner's name is engraved on each vessel, which can be borrowed by any member of the association under which they are organized. During the wedding season a good *waza* can earn 10,000 rupees (*c.* £600) a month. Their lean time is Ramazan, the month of fasting.

I arrived early at the Abdulla house to watch the *wazas*. The air was rich with the aroma of saffron being crushed, packets of cumin, cardamom, cinnamon and cloves being opened and red peppers being pounded. Eight male sheep had been slaughtered. Their rib cages were boiled in cauldrons with spices and salt, then cut and deep-fried to become *tubbak mans*. Other parts, from the backbone to the back-strap, were tossed into big vats of boiling salted water and made into a variety of dishes. The broth became *yakhni* or stock, and two kinds of curries were cooked, flavoured with the famous saffron from Pampur. Chopped bits of mutton were mixed for the cigar-shaped *seikh kebabs*. Four men pounded meat for the *pièce de résistance* of the meal, the golf ball-sized *gustaba* and *rista*, served respectively in a creamy sauce and a pepper-red curry. The fineness of the pounded meat would show the *waza*'s art. Any taste of membrane or sinew would bring the chef down a notch. A spiced sauce called *aab ghosta* was prepared from a mixture of tail and backbone meat with yoghurt and *yakhni*. There was also tripe with saffron, eggplant in a pungent gravy, and *phirni*, a dessert of vermicelli, crushed almonds and milk. Rice was steamed in huge vessels to satisfy over a hundred hungry guests.

When lunch was served, the men, wearing Western suits and *achkans* (knee-length Nehru coats), and the bejewelled women, in saris and satin *pherans*, sat on carpets four to a platter in segregated sections. The chief guest, Sheikh Abdullah, and his party were led to the living room. There they ate the *wazwan*, including a delicacy, the tails of the sheep. Showing his gusto, the Sheikh downed a tall tumbler of the rich *aab ghosta*.

I left the Vale the day after this splendid feast. The Airbus was packed with tourists who had come to see the land of the *Nīla Nag*, the Lord of the Snakes. As the aircraft took off, I spotted the village of Wathore and the tiny figures of my folk-theatre friends and other farmers pounding paddy. The dying chinar leaves wore their rust-red autumn colours, signalling the advent of winter. As I said a silent farewell, the dark shadow of a different kind of change crossed my mind. Would the Bhands, the Sufis and the shrines survive? Or would the laughter, the music and the mimicry of the histrionic Kashmiris die – the victim of the fundamentalists slowly spreading venom? If that ever happens, Kashmir will be India's paradise lost.

Captions

1 A farmer who lives on the island in the background is dredging Dal Lake's rich loam for use in his vegetable garden.

2 Two women collecting lotus leaves for cattle fodder, Dal Lake.

3 A farmer and his wife tend their floating vegetable garden, Dal Lake.

4 A Moghul rampart extending from Hari Parbat, Akbar's fort (not seen), to the blossoming almond trees above Nagin Lake.

5 A pear tree flowers in a field through which a farmer is heading for home, on the road to Tsrar Sharif.

6 Transplanting paddy, on the outskirts of Srinagar.

7 A paddy harvest in the autumn, near Achabal.

8 Spring mustard fields; farmers' families are embroidering and one man puffs at a hubble bubble. Tar from road-works smears stones near Harwan.

9 An English lesson in an open-air Jamaat-i-Islami (fundamentalist Moslem sect) school, Ganderbal village.

10 A boy removes the canvas cover from his father's car. In the background, the grass-covered shrine of Madin Sahib, built 1438, Srinagar.

11 The white wooden horse was a joke-present from one polo-playing Maharaja (Jaipur) to another (Kashmir). A White Horse whiskey dealer rescued it from a junk heap and installed it in front of a building in Srinagar which he rents to a bank.

12 Srinagar and the Jhelum River seen through a maze of windows.

13 The driver of a three-wheel scooter taxi, and a shop selling copper and aluminium utensils, Srinagar.

14 Fruit-seller and a boy with a child at Zaina Kadal Bridge, Jhelum River, Srinagar.

15 Woman passerby and man holding yarn, Zaina Kadal, Srinagar.

16 Textile merchants, Zaina Kadal, Srinagar.

17 Kashmiris outside a village circus near Traal.

18 Boys selling lotuses in front of a tourist car, Nishat garden.

19 Migrant postcard sellers from India in Srinagar.

20 Skull-cap maker in his shop and workplace, Srinagar. The doors advertise a Bombay movie.

21 Hawkers in boats sell lotus leaves for cattle fodder, Puz Mohalla Moghul Bridge, Srinagar.

22 Vegetable market, Dal Lake.

23 Mother and daughter rowing to their island home, Dal Lake.

24 Kashmiri boys fishing in Nagin Lake, lined by houseboats – Kashmir's floating hotels.

25 Dunga boats in Jhelum River, Srinagar, models for the houseboats developed by the English. The Hindu temple in the background catches the evening light.

26 Floating garden pulled by boatmen from Nagin to Dal. Gardens are staked to the beds of lakes.

27 Beehives in springtime, Hari Parbat hill.

28 In spring, farmers tend an almond orchard near the village of Nagan.

29 A farmer breaks for lunch with his wife and mother; Pohor River area.

30 Girls running to work in the mustard fields in the outskirts of Srinagar.

31 Mud and thatch-roofed houses, Naulora village.
32 Chillies drying in autumn, Naulora village.
33 Farmers make bricks, while one man prays to Mecca and another tends sheep, near Wular Lake.
34 Farmers after prayers, near Sopore.
35 Apples being gathered in an orchard, near Sopore.
36 Saffron flowers being plucked, near Pampur.
37 At the shrine of Baba Shakrudin, a woman carries a hen and, on her head, a sack of rice for feasting.
38 Children on a crude carousel during a festival at the shrine of Avantipur.
39 Pottery sellers at the shrine of Hazratbal on the Prophet's birthday.
40 Dard Paither, folk theatre, Wathore village. The Dard king is flanked by two queens acted by men.
41 Gossain Paither, Wathore. The play satirizes Hindu holy men making the pilgrimage to Amarnath Cave.
42 Dumbali dance, Wathore.
43 Rose petals showered on bride and groom (behind tray), Srinagar. The couple symbolize the god Siva and his consort Parvati.
44 Pandit (Hindu) wedding ritual.
45 Moslem wedding near Baramulla. The bridegroom wears a garland of money.
46 Gujars (mountain farmer-herders) sip Kashmiri tea around a stove, at the anniversary of a death, Sind Valley.
47 Sufiana Kalam ("music of mystic contentment"): master musician Mohammed Ghulam Qaleen Bhaff, with his son playing the zither-like santoor, Srinagar.
48 Sufi gathering in the town of Tsrar Sharif.
49 A saffron merchant in a Pampur home.
50 A weaver in the Trans-Asia carpet factory, Srinagar.
51 Gubba (blankets) being embroidered by two men, Anantnag.
52 Girls at a papier-mâché school in Srinagar.
53 Papier-mâché master, Ghulam Hussain Mir, sick in bed, with unfinished screens against the wall. His grandson sits by the wicker-work kangri which holds live coals, Srinagar.
54 After prayers at a mosque in Srinagar named after the Sufi saint Shah Hamadan.
55 Watermelon seller and clients, Jhelum Bridge, Srinagar. Namdas (woollen mats and floor coverings) are drying on the railing.
56 Men and woman unload hay from barges, Jhelum River.
57 Boys with a kite, and namdas being dried, Srinagar.
58 Pedestrians pass road-building machinery in front of Srinagar's exhibition grounds.
59 A horse which collapsed while pulling a cart loaded with rice flour sacks, Puz Mohalla Bridge, Srinagar.
60 The preparation of wazwan, the elaborate Kashmiri meal.
61 Some of 20,000 Hindu pilgrims making their annual visit to Amarnath Cave to worship Siva on

Sawan *(July–August) full-moon day. On the bottom left corner,* Amaravati, *or Immortal Stream.*

62   *Amarnath pilgrims at Sheshnag Lake.*

63   *Pilgrims rest after worship at Amarnath Cave.*

64   *Amarnath pilgrims approaching 14,000-foot Mahagunas, the highest point on the pilgrimage.*

65, 66   *Bakharwals (goat-herders) migrate every summer from the Jammu hills to high Kashmiri mountain pastures. Here, in autumn, they are on their way out of the Vale.*

67   *Sun Temple at Martand, near Anantnag, built by Lalitaditya (724–61).*

68   *A gardener decorates Nishat Bagh (Garden of Gladness); niches below a waterfall.*

69   *A woman sweeping up autumn leaves, at Patan, for burning in wicker-work braziers, or kangris.*

70   *A Kashmiri family picnics at Nishat Bagh, a major Moghul garden.*

71   *An immense tree trunk at Nishat Bagh.*

72   *Gardeners and tourists on a terrace at Nishat Bagh facing Dal Lake.*

73   *Nishat in spring.*

74   *Shalimar garden with chinar, or Oriental plane trees. It was built by Jehangir, early seventeenth century.*

75   *Indian tourists at Shalimar.*

76   *Wular Lake in the spring. The shrine of Baba Shakrudin crowns the hill in the background.*

77   *A peach tree flowering at the seventeenth-century Pari Mahal (Fairies' Palace).*

78   *Wular Lake, with a villager and a flight of birds.*

1

3

4

5

9

14

15

18

19

20

22

42

45

48

49

50

54

58

63

65

71

73

77

78